honor and reward in fulfilling this office. The wealth of Bible references in the book will implement its further use as a hand-book for study of the Bible as related to the responsibilities of leaders in the church.

Paul S. Wright

Born of American Presbyterian missionary parents in Iran, Dr. Wright was educated at Wooster College, Ohio (B.A.), and McCormick Theological Seminary, Chicago, Illinois (B.D.), and holds the honorary degrees of D.D., LL.D., and Doctor of Humane Letters. He has served pastorates in Crosby and Bismarck, North Dakota; Minneapolis, Minnesota; and Oklahoma City, Oklahoma. Pastor of the First Presbyterian Church, Portland, Oregon, since 1941, Dr. Wright was Moderator of the Presbyterian Church in the U.S.A., 1955–1956.

THE DUTIES
OF THE
RULING
ELDER

THE DUTIES
OF THE
RULING
ELDER

by Paul S. Wright

Philadelphia

THE WESTMINSTER PRESS

Library of Congress Catalog Card No.: 57–10765

PRINTED IN THE UNITED STATES OF AMERICA

CONTENTS

FOREWORD

THIS BOOK has long been needed. It answers in a most effective way the real questions that may be asked concerning the office of ruling elder. The wealth of its Biblical references makes it a book that merits not only a quick reading but also use as a handbook for a considerable study of the Bible as related to the responsibilities of leaders in the church.

THE DUTIES OF THE RULING ELDER is an ideal book to put into the hands of any man who is considering whether he will accept nomination to be a ruling elder in one of the congregations of the Presbyterian Church. It is written by a pastor who, in years of experience, has counseled with many men in this position; and I hope that many churches will make it possible for all their prospective elders to read this book. It will, of course, be equally valuable for elders just beginning and for those already serving. It will help them to re-examine their attitudes and sense of responsibility in their office.

— EUGENE CARSON BLAKE

INTRODUCTION

YOU have been elected a ruling elder in the Presbyterian Church. Doubtless many questions thrust themselves upon you when you were asked if your name might be presented to the congregation for election to this office: " I wonder if I'm the right person? What is a ruling elder? How did it happen that the Presbyterian Church has ruling elders? What do they do? How much time will it take? " This does not exhaust all that you wanted to know about being a ruling elder. You consented, however, to your election because you strongly believe in the church and want to do your part in its service.

This book is intended to help you to enjoy your duties and to perform them effectively. It will be a sort of manual, such as comes with the purchase of a new car. The fun, of course, is not in reading the manual but in driving the car! Yet for a novice who does not know automobiles some knowledge about the cars is necessary for enjoyment in driving it. So, too, it is hoped that reading this book may help you

9

to find increasing satisfaction in your service to the church.

There will be much that you may wish to know concerning the office of ruling elder that you will not find here. This is not an encyclopedia on the subject! There is much more that you will learn during your term in office.

The Presbyterian Church is convinced that an effective lay leadership is God's will for his church and essential to its spiritual vitality. Consequently, to train such a leadership is a priority. Splendid materials for this purpose have been prepared for use by ministers and ruling elders. So, one of the alluring prospects to which you may look forward is the opportunity for self-improvement and growth through study courses and training experiences in which you will participate with other ruling elders who will be serving with you.

Yours is an important job. The Presbyterian Church holds it in honor. May you find increasing joy in the performance of its duties, and may you be a faithful servant of our Lord Jesus Christ.

I
GOD CALLS LAYMEN
TO SERVE

YOU ARE a Protestant and a Presbyterian. This fact makes a big difference when you, as a layman, define your position in the church. You may have taken it quite for granted that you are teaching in the church school, or participating in committee work which determines the program of your church, or assisting your minister in parish visiting, or performing many other duties necessary to the efficiency and well-being of your church. You may even have conducted divine worship when your minister was away or on Laymen's Sunday when attention is given to the unique relationship between the man in the pew and his church. Whatever part you may have taken in the life of your church, you have correctly assumed that because you are a Christian you have a right, indeed a duty, to be more than a spectator while " professionals " perform all important functions, or a passive recipient of moral and spiritual instruction as authoritatively given by ecclesiastics. In a very real sense the laymen are the church!

Let us press this thought a little farther. Is the distinction that we commonly make between laymen and professionals valid in religion as in other fields? Certainly in medicine or law or engineering it is right to differentiate between laymen and professionals. In these and in many other vocations we need specialists who have technical knowledge and skills that the rest of us do not possess; and we would be foolish not to avail ourselves of the competence that is theirs. But is this true also in religion?

The Roman Catholic Church believes and teaches that this distinction must be recognized within church order also. It claims that Christ himself has created two classes of believers: one a clerical class with unique status in relation to God, and the other a lay class which stands in quite a different and inferior position ecclesiastically and functionally. According to this concept of church order there are gradations of spiritual authority beginning with the pope, who is supreme, and descending by degrees to the parish priest. Through the rite of ordination each priest is initiated into the succession of the apostles whom Christ appointed, so it is claimed, in order that the church might be infallibly guided in all that pertains to right doctrine and moral living. Theirs is a priestly office which no member of the congregation may perform; through them Christ exercises his rule in the church. They are invested with the power of the keys to open or to close the gates of the Kingdom of Heaven. All this is a divine provision for the proper government of the church and for the nurture and assurance of the flock of God. As the people unquestioningly believe the doctrine that is taught them by the priests and faithfully obey the will of God as interpreted by the church, they will be saved.

It is obvious that this is not the concept or practice of the Protestant Church, and in particular it is not the way of the Presbyterian Church. Superficially it may appear that we too have two classes in the church — ministers and laymen. Ministers are required to fulfill certain academic requirements — four years of college and three years of theological studies. They are then ordained by the presbytery and perform certain duties in the church which other members of the congregation do not; in particular they preach the Word and administer the sacraments as well as moderate the session. Laymen may sometimes speak from the pulpit, but they do not fulfill either of the last two functions. Also ministers seem to wield an authority that none of the parishioners exercises. Are we, then, merely quibbling when we claim a difference between Protestants and Roman Catholics regarding the status of clergy and laity in the church?

The difference between us becomes clear on three counts:

1. Protestants insist that priesthood is an office of every member of the church and not only of a special order. Each believer is his own priest. He may come to God without benefit of clergy because Christ is his

Mediator. He may make confession and receive forgiveness by that right which his Lord has bestowed upon him. In all fairness to the Roman Catholic Church it must be stated that it does not claim that the priest has power to forgive sin but only has authority from the church to hear confession and in the name of Christ to give assurance of pardon. But it is just at this point that the priesthood of all believers gains deeper meaning; for every Christian ought to be not only his own priest but to serve the priestly office to his fellows. In his pastoral letter James exhorts believers to " confess your sins to one another, and pray for one another, that you may be healed " (James 5:16). Each person who is himself a forgiven sinner may be the channel of God's grace to a fellow sinner seeking the Father's forgiveness and peace. This wonderful service may be performed more effectively often by a spiritually experienced Christian who is a friend than by the minister. Ideally it ought never to be necessary for a layman to say to another person seeking religious help, " You had better go to the minister." By his calling to be a Christian he has that privilege himself.

The priesthood of all believers underlies the worship of a Protestant church. Worship is a corporate act in which each participant helps his fellow. This is particularly evident in the observance of the Lord's Supper. The minister presides at the Lord's Table, but Christ himself is present as host. The minister has no power to change the elements of bread and

wine into the flesh and blood of Christ; in the name
of the people he sets these apart by prayer and thanks-
giving for a sacred use. Then he passes these " signs
and seals " of the redeeming death of our Lord to the
ruling elders, who pass them to the people, each person passing them in turn to his neighbor. This is a
moving dramatization of the truth that we have one
Master and we all are brethren. As each communicant
partakes of the bread and wine, he is led by the Holy
Spirit to discern the Real within the symbol, to offer
his own need to God and to receive personally the enabling grace. The emphasis is not upon what a priest
or minister does, but upon the conversation between
each soul and Christ really present to him by faith.
Thus in partaking of the elements each man is priest
to himself; and in passing them to his neighbor and
in his prayers for others, he is priest to his brethren.

While the Lord's Supper is the clearest instance of
how worship is based upon the priesthood of all believers, this doctrine is reflected in every other act of
worship. Martin Luther observed that congregational
singing is a priestly service in which each worshiper
helps his fellow man to praise God. A friendly greet-
ing at the close of service brings a stranger within the
embrace of Christian friendship and is certainly a
means of grace. Leading the family in worship is a
privilege by which the father may be priest within his
own household. Especially in the life of prayer may
every believer use his God-given power and right that
" so the whole round earth is every way bound by gold

chains about the feet of God." When we are what we ought to be, every believer in Christ is one through whom men may come to God and God's grace may be given to men. You see what a privilege and responsibility inheres in our call to be disciples of Jesus Christ.

2. A second distinguishing position of Protestantism is its concept of ordination and the ministry. Since we are Presbyterians, let us confine our thought to our own church system. By "ordination" we refer to a religious rite practiced certainly from very early times in the Christian church. (Acts 6:6; 13:3; I Tim. 4:14; 5:22.) It is based upon the conviction that the Holy Spirit bestows gifts upon various persons for the common good (I Cor. 12:4–11). In acknowledgment of God's call and enduement of these persons, they are set apart, through the laying on of hands, to those offices in the church for which their several gifts particularly fit them. According to the Form of Government of our church (Ch. VII, Sec. 2), "the ordinary and perpetual officers in the church set forth in the New Testament are bishops or ministers and ruling elders and deacons" (I Tim. 3:1, Eph. 4:11–12; I Tim. 5:17; Phil. 1:1). All who hold office in these orders are ordained persons who perform particular functions in relation to the various needs of the people of God.

Of bishops or ministers (we hold these terms to be interchangeable but by common usage prefer the lat-

ter) the Form of Government states: " The office of
the ministry is the first in the church in both dignity
and usefulness. The person who fills this office has, in
Scripture, obtained different names expressive of his
various duties. As he has the oversight of the flock of
Christ he is termed bishop. As he feeds them with
spiritual food he is termed pastor. As he serves Christ
in the church he is termed minister. As it is his duty
to be grave and prudent, and an example to the flock,
and to govern well in the house and kingdom of
Christ, he is termed presbyter or elder. As he is sent
to declare the will of God to sinners, and to beseech
them to be reconciled to God through Christ, he is
termed ambassador. And as he dispenses the manifold
grace of God and the ordinances instituted by Christ,
he is termed steward of the mysteries of God. Both
men and women may be called to this office." (Ch.
VIII, Sec. 2.)

Of ruling elders, the Form of Government declares: "Ruling elders, the immediate representatives
of the people, are chosen by them, that, in association
with the pastors or ministers, they may exercise government and discipline, and take the oversight of the
spiritual interests of the particular church, and also
of the church generally, when called thereunto."
(Ch. IX, Sec. 4.) Of deacons it says " The Scriptures
clearly point out deacons as distinct officers in the
church. The office is one of sympathy and service,
after the example of the Lord Jesus." (Ch. X, Sec. 1.)

Since our interest at the moment is in the two orders — the ministry and the ruling eldership — let us note a few points of similarity and of contrast.

Of ministers it is stated that they are " to govern well in the house and kingdom of Christ " and so are termed presbyters or elders. This work they share with the ruling elders who, in this regard, have a standing in the church equal with ministers. The vote of a ruling elder in presbytery, synod, or General Assembly counts for just as much as that of a minister. In the General Assembly there are an equal number of ministers and ruling elders, and in presbytery and synod the number of ministers and ruling elders is approximately equal. Such considerations make it obvious that there is not a sharp distinction between the clergy and the laity in the Presbyterian Church. On the contrary there is a significant parity between them, and that in a very important area of the church's life.

But there is also difference. Ruling elders " do not labor in the word and doctrine." This is required of the ministry, and if it is to be done in such a manner as shall " rightly handle the word of truth," it calls for adequate training and faithful preparation (II Tim. 2:15) . A minister ought, therefore, to be much better skilled than are most laymen in preaching the Word of God. Indeed, if he is a true minister he will have been called by the Holy Spirit to this vocation and his academic discipline is intended only to make him a worthy workman. So by divine call and by training he has a position of unique importance and responsibility in relation to the flock of Christ. This is emphasized in the statement quoted above that " the office of the ministry is the *first* in the church in both dignity and usefulness." " Dignity and usefulness," it must be clearly understood, do not rest in a spiritual attribute or power possessed only by the minister through ordination, but derive wholly from the nature of the work to which his Lord has called him and from his more adequate training for it. Again we must remember, Christ is our Lord, and we all are brethren.

3. Our concept of religion also causes us to take a dim view of professionals and specialists in matters of Christian faith. Real religion is vital encounter with the living God. The truth of Christian faith is not some secret learning to which only ecclesiastically qualified men have access, nor a spiritual power which only certain persons can transmit. The heart of our religion is the risen Christ disclosing himself to persons whom his Spirit has awakened to faith. In all experience that is genuinely religious, it would be a perversion to think in terms of " professionalism." We should not tolerate professional pray-ers any more than we approve professional lovers! We must be very clear that when the church is its true self there are not two classes of people — one a professional class with a unique status in relation to God, and another a lay class which stands in a quite different and inferior position. Let us now rapidly scan the history of the Christian church so that we may see how from its

beginning laymen have been inherently a part of its order and life.

When we turn to the New Testament we find full warrant for the conviction that God's purpose is to use lay people to do his work in and through the church. Inevitably we think first of the people whom Christ chose to be with him. None of them were ecclesiastics! Peter was a fisherman; Matthew was a taxgatherer. Except for Nicodemus, no rulers of the synagogue or temple priests are mentioned among his followers. It is significant that those whom he called to participate in his mission were devout laymen. He sought men with a capacity for growth and for heroic loyalty, men who were willing to give themselves courageously in a spiritual venture. It is another instance of how God on occasion has had to bypass the " established " church and its leaders to get on with his purpose in the world. With few exceptions, the prophets of the Old Testament were laymen whom God called to put Israel right. Why is it that in matters of faith an institution may become a petrified mummy? Only openness of heart to the Spirit of the living God can keep a church vital. That openness of spirit Christ looked for and awakened in men. That was the credential for fitness for his mission.

After his death and resurrection, Christ's disciples met together without much organization in the community of believers. Peter seems to have been their spokesman, and we read of his prominence in the church in the early days in Jerusalem. When Peter

began his missionary journeys, James, the brother of
our Lord, assumed the leadership of the Christian
community in the Holy City. At the beginning the
company of believers did not distinguish themselves
from the Jewish people. They worshiped in the Temple and doubtless attended the synagogues. As they
multiplied and were scattered everywhere, and as the
synagogues began to exclude them from fellowship,
Christians became more conscious of their separation
from Judaism and more aware of their identity as a
new faith. The strong leadership of Paul and the
rapid spread of the Christian faith among the Greeks
hastened this process. Consequently, the small communities of Christians in the cities of the Roman Empire began to organize themselves. The pattern they
naturally would follow would be that of the synagogue with which they were familiar.

The synagogue was a very democratic institution.
It was not dominated by a "priestly" class or by a
hereditary succession of officers. Its origin dates to the
time of the destruction of the Temple and the cap-
tivity of Israel in Babylon. It came to have such importance among the Jews scattered in communities of
the Roman Empire that even after Temple worship
was restored in Jerusalem, these synagogues continued
to foster the religious life of Israel. Mention is frequently made in the New Testament of the " elders of
the synagogue." These were probably older men of
the community whose prestige among the people elevated them to positions of trust and oversight. Age

does have its advantages! Thus the office was designated by the age of those who occupied it. This was true also of the Roman senate, of the Greek Areopagus, and a custom everywhere practiced in early times when the rulers of the people, judges, and so forth, were selected from the elderly men. In course of time the term became a title regardless of the age of the person.

When Christians became separated from the synagogue and formed communities of their own, they patterned both their worship and their organization after the parent who had disowned them. Thus as there had been elders in the synagogue who were entrusted with the rule and order as well as the teaching of the people, so in the early Christian communities elders were appointed by the founders of the churches or chosen by the people themselves. The responsibilities of these men were particularly heavy and their work was the more valued where numbers of converts were made among the Greeks. Congregations were not yet large enough to have settled " ministers." It seems that apostles (really missionaries) , preachers, and teachers went from place to place each performing a helpful service. When they were not present, however, the discipline and nurture of the company of the faithful was in the hands of the elders. Naturally they came to be persons highly esteemed and invaluable to the church. The measure of respect and confidence in which the apostle Paul held them is evident in the touching story in The Acts where he

summoned the elders of the church in Ephesus to
Miletus for a conference and a parting word (Acts
20:17–38). How much the church owed in those early
days to the wisdom and fidelity of the ruling elders
can never be measured. Suffice it to say that it was this
noble company who preserved in large part the in-
tegrity of the faith and in times of persecution rallied
the flock to withstand the blow.

In the centuries that followed, this democratic, lay-
administered organization of the church disappeared.
For better and for worse there developed the hier-
archal structure which still characterizes the Roman
Catholic Church. The administration of the church
and its work of preaching, teaching, and worship were
all performed by the clergy. The people were bene-
ficiaries of spiritual treasures dispensed by the priests.
The consequence was an unhappy exclusion of the
laity from all responsible participation in and direction of religious activities. But laymen may be more
genuinely spiritual than priests and their will to serve
Christ as determined as that of prelates! So there arose
certain lay orders within the church which fostered
a life of piety and good deeds. The most heart-warm-
ing chapters of church history are those which tell the
story of these communities of humble faith and service which kept alive the spiritual glow in an institution that had largely lost religious vitality.

At the beginning of the sixteenth century the time
was ripe for change. A mighty religious movement,
known as the Reformation, swept Europe. Its purpose

was not to start a new church but to cleanse the exist-
ing church of impurities and abuses. It was sparked
by the rediscovery of the faith of the early Christians,
to which the New Testament bore witness. For our
present purpose we shall confine our story to the Reformation in Geneva, Switzerland, of which John Calvin was the leader. The beginnings of the Presbyterian system of doctrine and church government lie
there.

For his model John Calvin did not go back to the
very early apostolic church, but to the church of the
second century. Earlier we showed how there was little organization in the first companies of Christians.
By them it was thought that the Holy Spirit distributed gifts to various persons for the benefit of the
whole group (I Cor. 12:4–11) and the whole congregation assumed responsibility for its own order
and discipline. This situation changed early in the
second century. A better articulated system developed. Calvin assumed that Christ had instituted in
his church the four offices of pastor, teacher, ruling
elder, and deacon: pastors were to preach the Word
of God; teachers were to establish schools for the education of the young and for the instruction of adults
(the beginning of the public-school system and the
Presbyterian emphasis upon Christian education);
ruling elders to maintain order and discipline; and
deacons to administer charities for the poor. These
ruling elders were laymen, twelve in number, representing various parishes in the city and related to

both the church and the civic government. They took
an oath similar to that prescribed for the ministers.
They met once each week with the pastors in a body
known as the consistory to hear complaints against
immoralities, or indecent language, or doctrinal er-
rors, and any other matters that might corrupt the
purity of the church and bring reproach to its good
name. At the end of the year they must present themselves to the magistrates of Geneva, who decided
whether they had faithfully performed their duties
and should be kept in office!

Here we have the elements characteristic of Presbyterian ecclesiastical life and discipline. Ministers and
laymen with equal authority but with division of responsibility and labor serve the church for its edifica-
tion and order. When the Reformation spread beyond Geneva it was bound to undergo modification.
The civil authority would not be as closely related
jurisdictionally to the church, and the ruling elders
would be elected by members of the congregation and
not appointed from councils of the municipal government. Yet they continued to be entrusted with the
" peace, unity, and purity of the church," and so, in
differentiation from the pastors, were called " ruling " elders. From Geneva the Reformation spread to
Scotland, to north Ireland, to Holland, and from the
old world to the new. During this migration it never
lost its ecclesiastical structure. In any Presbyterian
church, of whatever size or locality, the session is the
superior authority charged with responsibility for the

whole life of the congregation; ministers and ruling elders — ordained men both — under the guidance of the Holy Spirit working together to " present every man mature in Christ " (Col. 1:28) .

II
WHO QUALIFIES
FOR ELDERSHIP?

PHIL was proud and happy that his church had just elected him to the ruling eldership. It was gratifying to him that this confidence had been placed in him. He had grown up in the church and his happiest experiences were associated with it. So he wrote at once to his mother to share the good news with her. She too was a sincere Christian. She had been raised in the venerable Scottish tradition of the Presbyterian Church where elders were reputed to be devout men of superior character and spiritual attainment. It came as a great surprise to her that her son had been elevated to this honorable office. In her reply to Phil she wrote, " Son, are you good enough to be an elder? "

At the time, he was twenty-eight years old. Perhaps his youth had something to do with his mother's qualms. As we have already noted, from earliest times in every society, the old men have been asked to give counsel and leadership to the people; hence the term " elder." Phil's mother may have doubted that he had learned sufficiently from experience the wisdom he would need for spiritual leadership.

But in this matter of age, society has completely changed its viewpoint! Old people sometimes complain that it has bypassed them and picked up young people hardly out of school for important positions. It can't be denied that the performance of youth, when they are the right kind of youth, is mighty convincing. In regard to being " good enough " for the eldership, years have relatively little to do with it. Right qualifications are not paced by the calendar. There are many fine ruling elders who exceed the Biblical " threescore years and ten," and there are also hundreds of splendid young men who are creditably discharging the duties of this office. Indeed, the church has found it to be greatly to its advantage to avail itself of the gifts and services that each may bring — " your young men shall see visions, and your old men shall dream dreams " (Acts 2:17).

Until comparatively recently men only were permitted by the Constitution of the Presbyterian Church to qualify for the eldership. After careful study of the Scriptures on this subject and earnest theological debate, the General Assembly approved an overture that opened the eldership to the election of women. With logical consistency, a later General Assembly approved an overture to amend the Constitution to permit the ordination of women as ministers; and the presbyteries ratified this amendment. The wisdom of this action in the first instance has already been amply demonstrated in the effective leadership that women have given to the church as elders. We are realizing the truth of the apostle Paul's statement that in Christ " there is neither male nor female; for you are all one in Christ Jesus " (Gal. 3:28). So we may set aside age and sex as factors that determine qualification for the office.

Of immediate pertinence, however, are two other considerations: (1) What must an elder *believe?* (2) What must an elder *be?* In this chapter we shall consider the first.

What Must an Elder Believe?

In accordance with the Constitution of the church, at the time of ordination of the ruling elder, certain questions are put to the candidate to which an affirmative answer must be given. The first three questions deal with one's personal religious faith, the last four with duties as an officer in the church (Form of Government, Ch. XVII, Sec. 7). A careful reading of the questions dealing with personal faith will indicate what an elder must believe.

The first question reads: " Do you believe in one God, Father, Son, and Holy Spirit — and do you confess anew the Lord Jesus Christ as your Savior and Lord, and acknowledge him Head over all things to the church, which is his body? "

Presbyterians, along with all other Christians whether Protestant, Roman Catholic, or Greek Orthodox, are monotheists and Trinitarians. By " monotheism " we mean that we conceive God to be one and not many. This belief we hold in common with Jews and Mohammedans also. And so we affirm that Father, Son, and Holy Spirit are not three gods, but one God. Yet Christians differ from other monotheists in their idea of the nature of the unity that is in God. It may seem ridiculous to assert that " three are one " and the easy way out of the Trinitarian dilemma may seem to be to affirm that God is one in the sense of a mathematical unit. Because the idea is hard and superficially illogical, there have been movements like the Unitarian, which have sought to remain within the church yet abandon the doctrine of the Trinity. But the history of the church manifests a stubborn refusal to compromise this issue and a determined insistence that within the unity of God there is a rich, if unfathomable, differentiation which we name " Father, Son, and Holy Spirit."

This doctrine is not the invention of fuzzy-minded theologians who love a mystery. In fact, no one invented it. It was formulated as the only adequate explanation for the total experience of men who had been confronted by the living God. The overpowering religious experience came first, then followed the effort to define that experience in terms of doctrine. There are depths in God which we shall never know, for finite creatures cannot possibly comprehend the Infinite and Eternal. Yet the revelation which God has made of himself in his dealings with mankind is authentic and many-sided. These are the data on which our idea of God rests. In trying to interpret them we arrive at the doctrine of the Trinity. It is thus the result of giving honest, intellectual formulation to our experience of God and not a logically conceived pattern of thought. The clue to understanding the doctrine is the question, " How has God actually revealed himself in human experience? " The Bible provides source material for an answer.

" In many and various ways God spoke of old to our fathers by the prophets." (Heb. 1:1.) God spoke not in audible words or in formulated communications but in mighty deeds. The revelation that God gave was not information about himself but acts in which his living presence was perceived by men the eyes of whose hearts had been enlightened (Eph. 1:18) by the Spirit of God. To them the creation spoke of " the glory of God " and the firmament showed forth " his handiwork " (Ps. 19:1) . His purpose was read in certain acts of history, particularly in the redemption of Israel from bondage in Egypt and the experiences incident to the settlement in Canaan. We have no universally convincing explanation why the prophets of Israel discerned in the events of their history the hand of God, the one Supreme God who created heaven and earth, all holy, all wise, and all just. We do not know how they came to believe that the destiny of their own people and of the world was in his will to rule in righteousness and mercy. What is clear is that this idea was firmly fixed in their view of things and explained for them the meaning of past events and of the future yet to be. Faith in the one true God inspired confidence in the covenant he had made with their fathers and expectation in his promise to bless them in a glorious age yet to dawn. This is what the writer to the Hebrews meant when he said that " God spoke of old to our fathers by the prophets."

He then proceeds, " But in these last days he has spoken to us by a Son, whom he appointed the heir of all things, through whom also he created the world." The writers of the New Testament were convinced that in telling the story of Jesus they were proclaiming the last of the mighty events of history in which the eternal purpose of God to visit and redeem his people (Luke 1:68) had transpired. They called their proclamation the " gospel " because it was the good news that in Jesus Christ the living God himself was present in their very midst bringing everlasting salvation. They did not write about Jesus as though he were another messenger who brought new tidings about God, although this is certainly in part what he did do; but they declared that in the person, the life, the death, the resurrection, and the ascension into glory of Jesus, God had achieved salvation, bringing reconciliation and triumph over sin and death. Jesus Christ was God's deed!

This experience was so overwhelming and indubitable that language was too poor a vehicle to express the joy and adoration awakened by it. " Blessed be the God and Father of our Lord Jesus Christ, who has blessed us in Christ with every spiritual blessing in the heavenly places." (Eph. 1:3.) " In this the love of God was made manifest among us, that God sent his only Son into the world, so that we might live through him." (I John 4:9.) " Blessed be the God and Father of our Lord Jesus Christ! By his great mercy we have been born anew to a living hope through the resurrection of Jesus Christ from the dead, and to an inheritance which is imperishable, undefiled, and unfading." (I Peter 1:3–4.) We might multiply these quotations indefinitely. They indicate not only the spirit of joy and triumph which pervades the New Testament, but point to its source in a salvation event that is inseparably united with the person and work of Christ. So possessed were they by the wonder of it and so engrossed in the proclamation of it, that they did not pause for theological reflection; that task was left for future generations of Christian thinkers. But a new dimension within the being of God had been opened to them in the person of his Son. Henceforth they would know God not only as the God of Abraham, Isaac, and Jacob but as " the God and Father of our Lord Jesus Christ " (Eph. 1:3) . In their minds and in their hearts, Jesus Christ and God were one within the bonds of a uniquely divine relationship.

The words in which they reported their experience and declared their faith might lead us to surmise that after his resurrection and ascension into glory, Jesus Christ was no longer among them. They preached that he was in heaven " seated at the right hand of

God." What they meant was that he had been elevated to a new status in the universe because he was " obedient unto death." He was given " the name which is above every name, that at the name of Jesus every knee should bow, in heaven and on earth and under the earth, and every tongue confess that Jesus Christ is Lord, to the glory of God the Father " (Phil. 2:9–11) . No longer was he the Suffering Servant of the Lord but the supreme Ruler and Determiner of destiny. Yet in ascribing to him this honor and power, they did not conceive of him as an absentee Ruler. On the contrary their deepest conviction was that " I am with you always, to the close of the age " (Matt. 28:20) .

His real but unseen presence with them they attributed to the sending of his Spirit. The Spirit was not to take the place made vacant by his assumed absence, but to enable them to realize precisely the opposite — that he had never left them. The Lord continued to be among his disciples, no longer in a visible body but in the reality of a spiritual presence. Through the Spirit he continued to teach them and to empower them for effective witness and right living. They believed that the Holy Spirit had been the means by which in former ages God had moved the prophets to discern his meaning in events and to declare his purpose to the world. The language of the writers of both the Old and the New Testaments would lead us to assume that they did not differentiate between their experience of God realized as actively present and the influence of the Holy Spirit. Yet the Holy Spirit is not confused with God, the Father, or Christ, from whom he is sent.

Thus we have a threefold experience which is yet one in that the divine is in every aspect of it. We shall not make sense of the doctrine of the Trinity unless we too have experienced God reconciling the world to himself in Christ and effecting reconciliation in our hearts through his Spirit. The logic of the doctrine is not a creation of man's mind but a deduction from a religious experience. We must choose between two ways by which we may try to understand the Christian affirmation regarding Father, Son, and Holy Spirit. One is to seek knowledge as to how the three Persons are related within the unity of the Godhead. Let it be frankly admitted that this is a mystery whose secret is not penetrable by finite minds. The other way is to begin with the actual revelation made to us of the nature of God and probe as deeply as we may the meaning for our lives of the fact that he has come as Father, as Son, as Holy Spirit. When we affirm that we believe this doctrine we are not claiming to understand the depths of God, but we are bearing witness that we cannot do justice to the rich and many-sided self-disclosure of God without it. Our knowledge of God has an analogy of sorts with our acquaintance with the moon: in both we may be familiar only with that face which is turned toward us. The other side of the moon, and of God, is hidden from us. We shall be content to live in the light that is vouchsafed us and worship Father, Son, and Holy Spirit, one God, blessed forever.

The second question concerns the Scriptures: " Do you believe the Scriptures of the Old and New Testaments to be the Word of God, the only infallible rule of faith and practice? "

Most of us have had difficulty in giving unqualified assent to this question. What stops us is the adjective " infallible." It may seem to many of us to imply too much. Yet we are puzzled how we can declare the Scriptures of the Old and New Testaments to be the Word of God without affirming that they are also without error. Some Christians do not find the claim to infallibility unreasonable and accept it without demur. Two considerations may help us in thinking our way through to an honest affirmation.

1. What do we mean by the " Word of God "? Certainly we do not mean in the first instance a written document or even a message audibly spoken and received. When the Bible declares, " The word of the Lord came to his prophet saying, . . ." usually there is no accompanying description as to how that word of God was received. Sometimes it was declared to have come in a vision, or a dream. Ancients believed that visions and dreams were mediums by which deity communicated to men. Almost invariably, however, the word of God came in connection with some important crisis in the life of a person or a nation. Reflecting upon experiences which are narrated in the Scriptures, we may infer that the word of God was

God himself actually active in a situation whose meaning was discerned by the prophet, himself a participant in it, by the work of the Holy Spirit. God " spoke " both in the event and in the heart of the prophet. What he " saw " or " heard " — that is, the divine significance in the revelation event — he preached as the word of the Lord which had come to him. In words, he declared " the Word " which he had seen. These words, when finally written down, form the Bible in part.

For all Christians, Jesus Christ is the living Word of God. In him the creative Word by which God made the universe, the eternal Reality which is the source of mind and freedom in man, was personally present. The Word of God is a Person. All that the New Testament says about Christ are words about the Word of God. So if we are thinking incisively and speaking accurately, we should differentiate between the Word of God and the Bible which is the book in which witness is given to it.

The last statement, however, must be qualified with a further observation. Except for the Old Testament we have no record of the actual way in which God has communicated his purpose and forwarded his will for man's redemption through specific acts related to the people of Israel; nor have we, except for the New Testament, any record of the continuation and climactic fulfillment in Jesus Christ of this same redemptive work of God. The relation between the Word of God and the Scriptures is not accidental; the living Word has awakened and inspired the writers of the Bible and has illumined the hearts and incited response in those who ever since have read it. So the Bible becomes for us also the Word of God. We may then confidently declare that we believe the Scriptures of the Old and New Testament to be the Word of God by which we know " what man is to believe concerning God, and what duty God requires of man.

How, then, may we interpret the further affirmation, " I believe the Scriptures . . . to be . . . the only infallible rule of faith and practice "? Let us note that the sphere in which the Bible is claimed to be infallible is in matters of " faith and practice." It does not infallibly inform us concerning science, history, geography, and so forth. But in the Bible we who are believers find a transcript of an authentic dealing with men by God whereby his true character is revealed and his grace and love are freely offered in Christ for our acceptance. The religion of the Bible is our religion; and we believe it to be final and real. Concerning the authenticity and validity of the self-imparting that God has made known through the Bible, the adjective " infallible " alone seems accurately descriptive.

We should realize, also, that when we speak of " infallibility " we do not imply that God has overbearingly forced us to accept by exercise of divine authority certain truths concerning religion. That is not the way God works. He does not violate the freedom with which he has endowed man. Rather, he works by way of persuasion, his Spirit leading man to accept as true what actually is true, and to discern truth as shining in its own light. So " infallibility " is not a description of how God works by his almightiness to safeguard his truth from any admixture of error, but of how he brings men through the gracious and patient work of the Holy Spirit authentically to know his will and to participate in his purpose. Christian faith and practice are thus in touch with "infallibilities," with God himself speaking to us; and the place in which he speaks to us is the Scriptures.

This question deals with what we accept as " the seat of authority " in religion. Truth alone is the supreme authority. But where are we to find that truth? For Protestants that truth is the living Word to which the Holy Scriptures testify. The living Word himself, who is God known to us in Jesus Christ through the Holy Spirit, stands above every other authority. By this Word the church is judged, under this Word alone man's conscience stands, and before him the world awaits its judgment. And the Bible is for us the supreme authority in all matters of faith and practice because in and through it the Word speaks as nowhere else. When an elder affirms belief in the Scriptures as the " infallible rule " he bows to its authority as supreme in Christian faith and conduct.

The third question reads: " Do you sincerely receive and adopt the Confession of Faith and Catachisms of this church, as containing the system of doctrine taught in the Holy Scriptures? "

When a person believes something clearly and strongly he ought to be able to put in words that which he believes. The Confession of Faith of the Presbyterian Church is an effort to spell out systematically what we as a church believe concerning God and concerning man in the light of God. Since the source of our knowledge and our authority in such matters is the Holy Scriptures, what is contained in the Confession of Faith is a statement of the faith we find in the Bible. Strictly speaking, the Bible is not a book of systematic theology. It is a story which tells how God has created the world, governs and sustains it, judges it, and in mercy offers it salvation. Theologians " systematize " what the story seems to imply. And this is what the Confession of Faith we receive does for Presbyterians.

It is called sometimes the " Westminster Confession of Faith." Its name is derived from a historic assembly which was convened by the English Parliament in Westminster on July 1, 1643. The Reformation had been carried to England and Scotland by men who had been driven into exile, and in Geneva had learned from the work of John Calvin a system of doctrine and order of church government which they wished to effect in the life of the church in their native land. The Parliament came under their influence and abolished episcopacy on the island. There was need as a consequence of this action for a new book of common worship, a new confession of faith, and a new form of church order. The overwhelming majority of the one hundred and twenty-one clergymen and thirty laymen who comprised the Westminster Assembly were Presbyterian Puritans. Scottish commissioners, without vote but with large influence, were also in the assembly. These men compiled a Directory for Worship, a Larger Catechism for pulpit exposition and a Shorter Catechism for the instruction of children, and a Confession of Faith, all of which were adopted by the General Assembly of the Church of Scotland and by the Parliament of England and continue to this day as the standards for Scottish and American Presbyterians.

The Westminster Confession and the Catechisms have always ranked among the most notable expositions of Calvinism. We may not agree with every statement they contain, but we may affirm that they do faithfully reflect the point of view of the Bible. All glory is attributed to God for the creation of the world and the salvation of his people. He alone is Lord of conscience and Sovereign over the nations of the world. All human enterprises must conform to his purpose and be subservient to his will. He has mercifully entered into a covenant of grace with his people whereby through Christ he will pardon their sins, faithfully guide and sustain them in this world, and victoriously lead them into his eternal Kingdom. The church is called into being by the preaching of his word and is indwelt by his Spirit that it may be a school of nurture in the knowledge of Christ, a worshiping fellowship of believers, a means for the propagation of the gospel, and an instrument of righteousness in the world. A thoughtful reading of the Confession of Faith will be a rewarding experience. No layman should be deterred by its seeming formidableness. Since it is a human document, the Presbyterian Church believes that it should be subject to change when need arises, and a procedure has been made by which changes can be instituted when presbyteries have given careful study to them and have signified approval by a two-thirds majority. But the Confession is so worthy a standard that it does not require frequent alteration. And that is proper for a creedal statement; it should be relatively classic and final in its conception and formulation, and yet flexible enough to be kept in touch with contemporary realities. The Presbyterian Church in the United States of America has issued a " Brief Statement of the Reformed Faith " which is printed in the front of *The Hymnal.* This statement is for the use of church members and summarizes succinctly what the Confession of Faith develops in fullness. Similarly, the United Presbyterian Church of North America issued *The Confessional Statement* in 1925. But elders are required to " sincerely receive and adopt " not just a shorter statement but the full and authoritative Confession of Faith as containing the system of doctrine taught in the Holy Scriptures. It should perhaps be said that a creed is not a strait jacket to bind our minds; it is a flag around which we may rally, a bulwark against false teaching, and an anchor to steady the church against being " carried about with every wind of doctrine " (Eph. 4:14) . When a church knows what it believes and can declare it clearly, it is in the strongest possible position to fulfill its Christ-given task.

III
WHAT MUST
AN ELDER BE?

FAITH and character are intimately related. What a person believes is reflected in his life, and conversely, what a person *is* has determinative influence on his faith. The life of a believer speaks far more convincingly than his words. And since " it is the duty of the elders to set the example of a godly conduct and character," it is all important that an elder shall be a worthy person. What shall we establish as a measuring rod to gauge fitness in terms of character?

Reflecting upon the men whom Jesus chose to be with him, we may be sure that many congregations would have passed them by as not coming up to the standard! There was Peter, emotionally volcanic, unpredictable, capable of fierce loyalty and sudden courage yet cringing before the scrutiny of a housemaid and violently denying his discipleship to Jesus, slow to overcome his prejudice against Gentiles, and vacillating in his conviction regarding the freedom and privileges of his new faith. There was Matthew, a taxgatherer, whose odious profession had dishonored him among his own people. Judas, as we know, had in him a fatal flaw which was not apparent on the surface of his life. These were not perfect men. Yet they were the persons whom Jesus chose, and what he was able to accomplish with and through them, both in his earthly life and by his Spirit after the resurrection, is a near miracle.

To take a single example, reflect for a moment what Jesus accomplished through Peter. The statemen made by Jesus and recorded in Matthew, "You are Peter, and on this rock I will build my church" (Matt. 16:18), while it cannot bear the weighty interpretation given it by the Roman Catholic Church, does indicate that Peter was given an important role in the leadership of the primitive church. In the early chapters of The Acts, which relate incidents that transpired in the Christian community immediately after the death and resurrection of Jesus, Peter acts as convener and spokesman for the group. Until he left Jerusalem on the apostolic mission of preaching, when James, the brother of the Lord, assumed his place, Peter was the central figure, wisely guiding the infant church through crises of internal friction and ably defending it against its adversaries. He did, indeed, become a rock in a crucial time when a less courageous and committed disciple would have failed the need of the hour.

This observation should encourage a person who is asked to be an elder not to decline the office because he may think himself unworthy. It is inevitable that **any man who is called by God to exercise leadership** in the church should hesitate to respond at once to the summons. The spiritual nature of the work makes demands which we feel unworthy to fulfill. This reaction is characteristic even of men in the Bible. When God summoned Moses from the burning bush to deliver his people from the hand of Pharaoh his reply was, " Who am I that I should go to Pharaoh, and bring the sons of Israel out of Egypt? " (Ex. 3:11). In the Temple, Isaiah had a vision of God from which he recoiled because the revealing light had exposed his soul: " I am a man of unclean lips, and I dwell in the midst of a people of unclean lips; for my eyes have seen the King, the Lord of hosts! " (Isa. 6:5). The word of the Lord came to Jeremiah, " Before I formed you in the womb I knew you, and before you were born I consecrated you; I appointed you a prophet to the nations." Jeremiah's immediate response indicated helpless unfitness: " Ah, Lord God! Behold, I do not know how to speak, for I am only a youth " (Jer. 1:4–10). But in the case of each of these persons the Lord gave reassurance that his enabling grace would make them useful in the service to which he called them. All of them did a conspicuous work for God.

So if our immediate reaction to being an elder might be expressed in the reply, " I'm not the man for the job; there must be others far better fitted for it," we are following a familiar pattern. But the matter should not end there; that's where a conversation begins in earnest! What personal qualifications fit one for the duties of this office? " Am I ' spiritual ' enough? " " I'm the ' trustee type '; I feel at home in the business world, and I am pretty confident in the sort of decisions and thinking that requires. But I'm uncertain about being an elder." " I believe in the church; but I'm not a person who prays a lot. Doesn't an elder have to do that? "

Perhaps we can arrive at a clearer understanding if we approach a consideration of the question under two heads: (1) the elder's qualifications as a Christian and a church member, and (2) his special qualifications as an officer of the church.

Qualifications as a Christian and a Church Member

We rightly assume that before a person can be an elder he must be a Christian. But it is difficult to define unambiguously what makes a person a Christian; either we are too arbitrarily sharp in drawing the picture or we are too vague. Christians are not easy subjects for portraits! Let us, nevertheless, make the attempt.

A Christian is a " committed " person. His life is not his own; he belongs to Jesus Christ. He is a person who has heard the message of God's love revealed in Christ and has realized that this love lays claim to the whole of himself. The apostle Paul expressed it as he pleaded earnestly with his readers: " I appeal to you therefore, brethren, by the mercies of God, to present your bodies as a living sacrifice, holy and acceptable to God, which is your spiritual worship. Do

not be conformed to this world but be transformed by
the renewal of your mind, that you may prove what is
the will of God, what is good and acceptable and perfect " (Rom. 12:1–2) . A twofold response is involved
in this appeal, both a firm initial decision — " present
your bodies as a living sacrifice " — and a consequent
development of life — " be transformed by the renewal of your mind." These are inseparably joined
to each other. We cannot " present our bodies as a
living sacrifice " without going on to a daily sur-
render of our minds and hearts to the Spirit of God
by which we come to see and feel and act from a point
of view very different from that which characterizes
the world that is not under the rule of Christ. Lest the
word " body " might confuse us, we should remember
that as the apostle intended it to be understood, much
more is implied than the physical body. He refers to
man's personality in its fullest and most effective em-
bodiment and expression; it is the " whole man " that
is to be laid upon the altar of dedication. Or we may
change the metaphor from sacrifice to citizenship.
When we understand our status as Christians, we shall
be aware that we have changed citizenship: our sub-
jection is no longer to the world of false ideals, wrong
objectives, and unworthy motives by which we were
once influenced; now our loyalty is to Christ and his
rule in all things. It is this decision to let the will of
God as it is revealed in Christ determine every aspect
of life that makes a person a Christian. It calls for
daily worship and obedience; it results in a trans-

formation of character whereby we are less and less imitators of " the Joneses " and more and more living expressions of God's Spirit.

A moment's reflection upon what has just been stated will make it evident that the qualification of an elder is not just that he is a good man, a rigorously ethical or even a kind and generous person, but he is also a Christian, and between the two there is a difference. The difference is a religious spirit. Many of our upright neighbors are model citizens in every respect, honest in business, cordial friends, community-minded, and strong advocates of clean living. But they lack, or have never cultivated, that which is essential in a Christian and in an elder — the awareness that a conversation takes place between man and God, and that on man's part that conversation leads to worship, to repentance, to challenge, and to commitment. A Christian may, or may not, be morally better than other men (we fervently hope that he will be!), but whatever he does he will do as in the sight of God. If he does wrong, it will not seem to him like breaking an impersonal traffic law, but he will confess with David, " Against thee, thee only, have I sinned, and done that which is evil in thy sight " (Ps. 51:4). For him sin is a personal breach of loyalty. By the same token " righteousness " is not primarily correctness of character, but grateful trust in God who loves him and resolute acceptance of God's will. Character should inevitably grow out of religious faith, but it is not the equivalent or the substitute for it. So being a religious man, an elder will wish to grow in his experience of God. Worship, both in private and with others, will be a valued practice for him; reading the Bible and other religiously creative literature will be included in his schedule; and his life will be a constant effort to give the Spirit control in all his words and deeds. There may be moments when he will despair of achieving any praiseworthy level of spiritual life; even Paul confessed that he had not " attained " (Phil. 3:12) . But he will be useful to God, nevertheless, if he persists as did the apostle when he wrote, " Forgetting what lies behind and straining forward to what lies ahead, I press on toward the goal for the prize of the upward call of God in Christ Jesus " (Phil. 3:13–14) .

Special Qualification as a Church Officer

Assuming that a person has a religious spirit which is expressed in a sincere life, what qualification beyond that is necessary for one elected to eldership? One would like to say, none! And this is right if we have mistakenly thought that there is an " elder type." The men who were chosen to administer charities in the early church are described in the book of The Acts as " of good repute, full of the Spirit and of wisdom " (ch. 6:3) , which implies that they were esteemed by the community, deeply and sincerely religious in spirit, and practical in judgment; surely, they would have been excellent elder material! Yet there is an unmistakable, if baffling, " something more " re-

quired in an elder. Let us try to describe it; it may all
add up to what we call " leadership."

An elder will work as a member of a team. He must
not, therefore, be an individualist in the sense that he
is inflexible and un-co-operative. He may be a person
of firm convictions and strong initiative, but his usefulness to the session and to the church will be dimin-
ished if these virtues lead to self-assertion or unbend-
ing insistence upon his own opinion. If this should be
his attitude, it ill comports with the spirit and form
of our church government. We have no bishops who
exercise authority over us in the name of Christ, and
no elder should assume this prerogative! We believe
that Christ rules us in a government " of the people,
by the people, for the people," his church. It is
our conviction that the Holy Spirit exercises leadership for the fullest advantage of the church when he
works through individuals as members of a group.
We base our government upon a Spirit-filled community, which chooses competent men who will represent them in the spiritual ordering of the church.
These are the elders who are responsible for the religious welfare and effective service of the congregation. When they gather as a session, they meet as
Spirit-filled men whose private judgments will be
either confirmed by the consent of the rest or cor-
rected in the light which falls from other minds. It
does not mean that the group is always right and that
the individual is always wrong; but the government
and discipline of the Presbyterian Church is firmly

based upon its faith that the Spirit of God speaks to and through the whole church, and not to special persons ecclesiastically qualified. This principle must also pervade a session meeting; and however right an elder may think he is, if his individuality disrupts the group spirit he is not helpfully fulfilling his office. To know how to think with others, pray with others, and work with others is an indispensable qualification.

In this relation mention should be made of the last question that a candidate for eldership is required to answer in the affirmative: " Do you promise to study the peace, unity, and purity of the church? " What is implied by each of these terms?

An elder is pledged to " study the peace . . . of the church." Our concept of peace is usually too negative, as though peace were only the absence of conflict. We are apt to think of it as a static condition in which all affairs go on without significant variation or change. With admittedly too little thought we are apt to think, for instance, that world peace is nations living quietly within fixed boundaries and molesting each other as little as possible. Actually that can never be in a world in which relentless change is the order of the day. We must visualize peace as dynamic, as purposeful and creative change. Eight cylinders under the hood of an automobile, perfectly synchronized and balanced, generating two hundred and fifty horsepower, is a picture of mechanical peace. Statesmen and businessmen of the world, retooling economic policies and revamping national and international agreements and laws in the light of changing conditions for the greater good of all, is a picture of world peace. The " peace . . . of the church " is the church in creative action as it earnestly seeks to understand its mission and fulfill it. So the session is not a body of officers pledged to resist change! A sleepy church must be awakened even if the session must provide the alarm to do it. Peace in the church is an alert congregation joyously and energetically fulfilling its mission as Christ's agent in the world. To study how this may be brought about is the concern of an elder.

Obviously there can be no peace where there is not unity. Paul the apostle pleads with the Christians at Philippi to complete his joy by " being of the same mind, having the same love, being in full accord and of one mind " (Phil. 2:2). He cites the example of Jesus as an incentive toward securing unity of spirit. As their Lord " emptied himself " of heavenly status and glory to take the form of a servant and even to suffer death upon the shameful cross for them, they must show a like spirit in doing nothing from selfishness or conceit, but in humility counting others better than themselves. Each should look not only to his own interests, but also to the interests of others. (Phil. 2:3–4.) No influence toward unity is more powerful in a church than this spirit demonstrated in the session. How sad is the misfortune where elders are divided from one another! Jealousies, ambitions, hurt feelings, party loyalties have then marred the unity which the Holy Spirit would engender among breth-

ren. It is equally sad when this division occurs between the pastor and the elders of the church. But it
need not continue long. God will send the spirit of
his Son into our hearts when we humbly pray for his
forgiveness and for reconciliation to one another in
him. Unity is his mind impressed upon ours and his
love shining in our hearts through the Holy Spirit.
No quarrels are quite so fierce and unrelenting as
religious quarrels because so much seems at stake. No
concern should lie closer to the heart of an elder than
" to keep the unity of the spirit in the bonds of
peace."

Lastly, an elder promises to " study the . . . purity of the church." This implies that the church may
be corrupted, and history confirms the sad truth. As
a watchman who defends the purity of the church, an
elder will stand guard at two approaches; for the
church may be corrupted in its doctrine; and the
church may be corrupted in its spirit. When these
bastions have fallen, it will also become corrupt in
practice.

As was said in the last chapter, the Presbyterian
Church is a creedal church and regards right doctrine
of great importance. For a believer the creed is a
road map — it helps him find his way. It is not the
way itself. The road is more important than the map,
admittedly; but without a map to indicate directions,
a traveler would be at serious disadvantage, and a
faulty map would be an unhappy deception. We believe that the way of salvation through Christ can be

described plainly enough in words that a seeker can be given indispensable help in his quest. This is the reason that we should be zealous for right teaching. But at this point a caution must be urged. Just as a road map must from time to time be revised to bring it into line with the real road (we shall not press this analogy any farther as to imply that the " way of salvation " ever changes), so theologies must be redrawn to bring them into conformity with a better understanding of God's dealings with us for our succor. Inadequate maps may be supplanted by better ones, and so it is with theologies. They are important, but they are man-made. So our attitude in the defense of pure doctrine will be a reverent and humble teachableness in the revelation of God's will with a firm purpose to understand and define it as clearly as possible. The Word of God speaking by his Spirit in the Holy Scriptures is our authoritative standard for purity of doctrine. Its message has been admirably set forth in the Westminster Confession of Faith and unites us in a declaration that is the same for all Presbyterian churches. To it, all teaching in our church must conform.

In the church's life, even more importantly than in its doctrine, the purity of the church must be defended. The church exists in the world, a world which the Scriptures warn us is both deceived and a deceiver. Jesus resisted its enticements to lead him from the path of devotion and obedience to the will of the Father, and challenged his disciples to make his conflict their own. The church is in the world, but the world must not be in the church. " Be ye holy; for I am holy," says the Lord.

This is not the place for a dissertation on worldliness, but a brief observation might be in order. In the memory of a good many of us worldliness consisted in dancing, playing cards, drinking, attending theater, profanity, Sabbath violation, and so forth. Purity in the church consisted in banning all such so-called evil practices. If this subject were brought up for discussion in session meeting, doubtless many attitudes would be expressed. Should young people hold dances in the church? How about old peoples' clubs meeting in the church as a service to the community where, as part of the program, cards are played? Should church members, and in particular elders, drink alcoholic beverages? On most questions of this kind sharp differences of opinion probably might be expressed; on some of them, however, there might be a unanimity of opinion.

We shall not discuss these questions helpfully unless we realize that worldliness is more subtle than any catalogue of questionable practices might indicate. If it consisted only of overt " sins," we should be more able to cope with its threat. There is vice enough in the church, God knows; and we should be deeply contrite whenever and wherever it appears among Christians. But relatively speaking, the church is probably as pure in this regard as it has ever been. Indeed, it is just the unimpeachable lives of most members that dull us to the real worldliness that blights us. Worldliness is the reign of the spirit of evil, as purity is the rule of the Spirit of Christ. " The kingdom of evil," writes John Oman, " is idolatry, so organized by hypocrisy that it is able to set itself up as the true order of the world. Valuing its neighbor only for itself, it makes possession the end and man the means, and turns the whole world into a temple for its idol, where it worships with all its mind and with all its heart and with all its strength. By the dazzling liturgy of all the worldly interests that appeal to selfish desire, it blinds its own eyes as well as the eyes of others, till its idol is accepted as the only true might in the world, over against which a rule of love seems mere fantasy and cloud-land. Nor did this idolatry ever erect a ritual so imposing as the material conquests of the present order of competition with its vast material equipment; nor was it ever so much taken at its face value as when thus enormously staged; nor has society ever been set by it on a more selfish foundation or been so robbed of the true uses of the world; nor has it ever issued in vaster destruction." (*Grace and Personality,* by John Oman. Cambridge University Press, 4th edition, 1931.)

Professor Oman's characterization of the kingdom of evil might well bear deep and frequent pondering by elders with immeasurable advantage to the purity of the church. When we say " our church is making progress," just what do we mean? The chamber of commerce has its standard for measuring growth; do we use the same in estimating the prosperity of a church? Too often we fail to distinguish between the world and the church, an easy oversight if the world is too much in the church. In essence they are so different that a man of the world must be born again to be a child of God's Kingdom.

How fully are elders ready to thrust the cross into their lives? There is death in the cross — death to self and the world. We who call ourselves disciples of Christ, dare we drink of the cup which he drank and receive the baptism wherewith he was baptized? That challenge we must face again and again, lest comfortably and interestingly we live a worldly life under the illusion that we are still Christians, that we are enjoying life eternal. May God spare us the easy pleasure of having escaped the shattering judgment of Christ's cross by which alone the sham of this world's pretension is exposed. The New Testament makes it clear that we shall never thrill to the joy of heaven who wish to possess the world and its fleeting satisfactions. " Purity of heart," a great Danish philosopher once said, " is to will one thing." " One thing have I desired of the Lord, that will I seek after," cried the psalmist. The church achieved purity through dedication to its crucified Lord.

It is holy to the degree that the Spirit of God overcomes the deceptions and bondage of the world and brings it into thralldom to the Reality that is in Christ. This condition an elder is pledged to endeavor to realize.

IV
THE SESSION

" THE session of a particular church consists of the pastor (or co-pastors) and the ruling elders in active service. . . .

" The session is charged with maintaining the spiritual government of the congregation; for which purpose it has power to inquire into the knowledge and Christian conduct of the members of the church; . . . to instruct parents who are communicants to present their children for baptism; to decide who shall be members of the church, and to receive them into the communion of the church upon profession of faith in Jesus Christ, upon presentation of satisfactory certificate of church membership, or, in the absence of such certificate upon the part of persons coming from other churches, upon reaffirmation of faith in Jesus Christ; to grant certificates of dismissal to other churches, which when given to parents shall always include the names of their baptized children; to admonish, to rebuke, to suspend or exclude from the sacraments, those who are found to deserve censure; to

59

concert the best measures for promoting the spiritual interests of the congregation; to supervise the church school, the work of the deacons and the trustees, and all the societies or agencies of the congregation; to participate with the minister in the examination, ordination, and installation of ruling elders and deacons on their election by the congregation; and to appoint representatives to higher judicatories of the church.

"Subject to the provisions of the Directory for Worship, the session shall have and exercise exclusive authority over the worship of the congregation, including the musical service; and shall determine the times and places of preaching the Word and all other religious services. It shall also have exclusive authority over the uses to which the church buildings and properties may be put, but may temporarily delegate the determination of such uses, subject always to the superior authority and direction of the session." (Form of Government, Ch. XI, Secs. 1, 6, 7.)

If you were about to attend a session meeting for the first time as a ruling elder, you would want to know what to expect when you arrived. Probably you would be well acquainted already with your fellow ruling elders; but if the membership of your church is large, you might not know all the persons present. One of the really rich satisfactions of being a ruling elder is the opportunity it gives for warm and valued friendships. Presbyterian men are not noted for bashfulness; so if someone is a stranger to you, do not hesitate to make his acquaintance! One of the finest contributions that a ruling elder can make to his church is the spirit of friendliness, and the session is a good place to start. Nowhere does the spirit of sincere comradeship pay larger dividends than in session meetings. " Where the Spirit of the Lord is, there is liberty." (II Cor. 3:17.)

The size of the session differs with each congregation and usually is determined both by the manner in which the congregation does its work and by the numerical strength of the membership. The Presbyterian Church insists upon the same form of government in each church but it does not specify the size of the session nor the way in which it shall be organized. These details are left to the discretion of each congregation and to the elders themselves who have been chosen by it to serve. The Form of Government stipulates that " two ruling elders, if there be so many, with the pastor, . . . shall be necessary to constitute a quorum." Evidently there have been, and are, churches that cannot muster two ruling elders! One may imagine appreciatively the faithful service such men have rendered in line of duty. Ordinarily, however, there will be several ruling elders and sometimes as many as fifty or sixty. To regularize for the entire church the provisions subject to which ruling elders are elected, the 1955 General Assembly proposed to the presbyteries a change in the Form of Government, which they approved. The amended form, put into effect by the 1956 Assembly, reads as follows: " No ruling elder shall be elected to the session for a term of more than three years, nor shall a ruling elder serve on the session for consecutive terms, either full or partial, aggregating more than six years. A ruling elder having been elected to the session for consecutive terms aggregating six years shall be ineligible to serve thereon for a further term until at least one year has elapsed from the expiration of the last term for which he was elected. A particular church may provide for a period of ineligibility after one full term. There shall always be three classes of ruling elders on the session as nearly equal in number as possible, one class only of which shall expire each year and terms shall always be for three years, except when it is necessary to elect some for shorter terms in order to equalize the numbers in the classes or to fill vacancies." (*Minutes* of General Assembly.) It is well to note that according to the rotation system, which is now the order for the Presbyterian Church U.S.A., no ruling elder who has been elected to the session for consecutive years aggregating six years is eligible for re-election until one year has elapsed from the expiration of the last term for which he was elected. A church may also, if it sees fit, make such a provision operative after fulfillment of three years' service. In either case the rotation system has certain advantages which are at once apparent: it makes it possible to elect to the session able men whose contribution might not otherwise be available, as well as to drop certain men when advisable without embarrassment.

Care must be exercised, however, not to abuse the system. It is not designed as a plan to make it possible for all the men of the church eventually to serve as ruling elders, nor does it imply that three or six years will be the total service that a ruling elder will give. The rotation system is intended to strengthen the session, and therefore the first consideration always is the fitness of the person to serve. If this consideration is undeviatingly the rule that controls use of the rotation system, it gives opportunity for effectively strengthening the session.

Your minister always will moderate the session. However, " when for prudential reasons it may appear inadvisable that some other minister should be invited to preside, the pastor shall, with the concurrence of the session, invite another minister belonging to the same presbytery to preside. In the case of the sickness or absence of the pastor, the same expedient may be adopted." There is no ambiguity in Presbyterian law that the moderator of the session shall be a minister, the only exception being in the case of the sickness or absence of the pastor, when " the session, the approval of the pastor first having been obtained, may convene and elect one of its own members to preside, except in judicial cases " (Form of Government, Ch. XI, Sec. 3) .

One may inquire why such a regulation was made. Probably one reason was to insure reverence and orderliness in the conduct of the spiritual affairs of the church; but since a ruling elder may, under certain circumstances, moderate the session, it is clear that a minister does not possess some ecclesiastical unction or status that qualifies him uniquely for this office. A deeper reason inheres in the very nature of the session itself. It is composed of the minister (or ministers) and ruling elders. Neither can function without the other: the minister cannot exercise authority in the church apart from the session; neither can the session act in an official capacity apart from the minister. Thus there are fused together the pastoral and teaching functions of the church in the person of the minister and the ruling aspects of church order in the persons of the ruling elders. Together they form, under Christ, the supreme authority in the local church charged with responsibility for the spiritual government of the whole congregation. And since " the office of the ministry is the first in the church in both dignity and usefulness " (Form of Government, Ch. VIII, Sec. 2), this status is acknowledged in the provision that " the pastor of the church shall be the moderator of the session " except for unusual circumstances when another minister, or in case of extreme inconvenience, a ruling elder may preside.

The minister convenes the session when he may judge it to be requisite; but usually it will meet at appointed times, perhaps regularly once each month, and on those occasions when new members are to be received or other matters require attention. He shall also always convene the session when requested by any two elders to do so. The presbytery, too, may direct that the session of any church under its jurisdiction shall convene. As is eminently proper when addressing itself to the Lord's business, meetings of the session always will open and close with prayer.

That the consideration of business shall proceed in an orderly manner, a docket should have been prepared. Usually this is done by the clerk in consultation with the moderator. It should anticipate all matters that need to come before the session. Since " the session is charged with maintaining the spiritual government of the congregation," various areas of responsibility ought to come regularly before it for prayerful consideration. The session should have as its aim and inspiration that which the apostle Paul declared to be his driving desire: "Him we proclaim, warning every man and teaching every man in all wisdom, that we may present every man mature in Christ. For this I toil, striving with all the energy which he mightily inspires within me." (Col. 1:28–29.) That is a big order and it calls for thoughtful planning and procedure that it may be carried into effect. The objective that should determine the whole life of the church is to produce a body of Christians " mature in Christ." The session is responsible for the progress of this work. Since also the local congregation is inseparably a part of the Presbyterian Church in its national scope and world-wide mission, phases of this wider relationship and work must receive due consideration.

A very useful little book, edited by the Stated Clerk of the General Assembly, gives a suggested docket for meetings of sessions, which can be modified as may best meet specific needs (*Presbyterian Law for the Local Church*, edited by Eugene Carson Blake) .

1. Opening prayer.
2. Calling of roll.
3. Reading and approval of minutes.
4. Communications from presbytery, synod, and General Assembly.
5. Reports of permanent committees.
6. Reports of special committees.
7. Report of pastor.
8. Report of clerk.
9. Report of treasurer.
10. Examination and reception of members.
11. Dismissal of members.
12. Arrangements for Lord's Supper when necessary.
13. Report to presbytery when in order.
14. Report of commissioner to presbytery or synod.
15. Unfinished business.
16. Miscellaneous business.
17. Adjournment.
18. Prayer and benediction.

Comments upon certain items of this docket may be helpful.

After the opening prayer, the first item of business will fall to the clerk of the session, who is appointed to his office by the session. His responsibility consists in keeping an accurate roll of attendance, recording the minutes of each meeting and of the annual meeting of the congregation, issuing letters of transfer when requested by members of the church and by the session, reporting to presbytery such information as it may seek and transmitting to the session communications from presbytery, synod, or General Assembly, and supervising the maintenance of the roll of church membership. Since it is his duty to keep accurate record of ruling elders attending each session, he will call the roll and report reasons for absence for those members not present. It is important that a ruling elder shall faithfully attend each session meeting, and it is expected of him when he cannot attend that he will so inform the clerk. When the roll call has been accomplished, the moderator will call upon the clerk to read minutes of the preceding meeting, which shall then be reviewed for accuracy and when found satisfactory shall be approved. The minutes of the session of each church are presented at least annually to the presbytery for examination. This obligation arises from the nature of government in the Presbyterian Church which rests authority over each session in the presbytery.

The docket also indicates reports of permanent and special committees. When a church is small and the session likewise is small, it may seem unnecessary to organize. It may be agreed that the session might better act as a committee of the whole. Following this pattern, the pastor would share with the ruling elders whatever matters were pertinent to the spiritual welfare of the people, and when decisions had been made as to courses of action, the matter could be referred to certain ruling elders best qualified to carry through specified parts of the program. This is a direct and simple way to get things done. Too often, however, it develops the unhappy situation in which the minister undertakes too large a share of the work, too much of the thinking and planning and carrying through. while the session tends to become a rubber stamp. There is also the likelihood that if the ball is tossed around only among the ruling elders and minister, the people themselves never get hold of it! It's not much fun playing a game in which one never handles the ball. The worst consequence is that, deprived of a chance to get in on the creative end of the work, members of the church will not grow " mature in Christ." The ideal fellowship is where every member of the church participates in some creative group experience. The session is not doing its work properly when it does all the work! It should divide, assign, and oversee the total program in which everyone ideally has a share. Even in a small church this division and assignment of responsibilities can be practiced, and in a large church it is imperative. This calls for appointment of committees.

Special committees, as the term implies, are those which are appointed for a specific and limited assignment, and upon the completion of it are dismissed. Permanent committees are assigned responsibility for various phases of the continuing program of the church. It should be borne constantly in mind that no two churches or communities are exactly alike. There is, therefore, no single committee structure that will work equally well in every place. The mission of the church is the same, but it will be variously performed in accordance with the factors peculiar to a given situation. A congregation in the heart of a great city and a church on the vast reaches of the Western plains could not possibly use the same form of organization. Yet sessions, whether of city or country churches, whether of larger or of smaller numbers, have identical responsibilities, and it should be possible to suggest some ideas of organization which might happily and imaginatively be adapted.

1. A prime responsibility of the session is to assist the pastor in the oversight of the spiritual welfare of the congregation. To perform this shepherding office, the session may well act as a committee of the whole. The end in view is such a church as that of which we read in the early chapters of The Acts of the Apostles: " And day by day, attending the temple together and breaking bread in their homes, they partook of food with glad and generous hearts, praising God and having favor with all the people. And the Lord added to their number day by day those who were being saved " (ch. 2:46–47) . They were drawn together by an experience of salvation in Christ which made them love one another. The apostle Paul referred to the church as the body of Christ in which each member had a distinct and important function. A strong sense

of unity pervaded the entire group. The church is more than a congregation of individuals; it is an organism in which every member finds meaning and usefulness in relation to the whole. This ideal the session must strive to achieve in each church; it is part of the meaning of the promise a ruling elder makes at his ordination " to study the peace, unity, and purity of the church."

In a small community, or church, where " everybody knows everybody " the care of the congregation may be relatively simple; new members will be made welcome, the sick will be remembered, and, in general, friendship will be encouraged among the people. In a large city, or in a large church, this will be a very heavy and a much-needed service. To carry it out effectively a plan should be devised by which each ruling elder is assigned a segment of the whole as his special concern. Sometimes this is accomplished by dividing the town or city into smaller parishes with a ruling elder, who may be assisted by others whom he may ask to help him, as leader of each group. He will thus be in touch with that portion of the parish which is assigned to him, using this intimate relationship in many helpful ways to report removals from the city and cases of illness or need, to assimilate new members, to arrange home meetings for prayer and discussion of the church program, and to give as much encouragement as he can to a warm personal relationship between members under his care. The service he may thus render is invaluable. Although a church may have several ministers, they cannot maintain this intimate relationship without the assistance of the ruling elders. Indeed, the pastor is greatly assisted in his own visiting if he can be informed by the ruling elders of people in need of his care.

2. " Subject to the provisions of the Directory for Worship, the session shall have and exercise exclusive authority over the worship of the congregation." (Form of Government, Ch. XI, Sec. 7.) Worship of God is the very heart of the Christian community. Many other services, once the sole concern of the church, have now been taken over by other agencies and organizations — education, philanthropies, healing — but worship remains the prime and indispensable function of the people of God. The session must be firmly convinced that public worship is supremely important. It will accordingly provide for this need and do all within its power to encourage the people to heed the admonition " not neglecting to meet together, as is the habit of some, but encouraging one another " (Heb. 10:25) . While elders may properly expect that the minister will be best qualified to lead congregational worship, it is by no means entirely his responsibility. If a minister is wise, he will seek the counsel and support of the session in this as in all other aspects of his ministry. The session should, therefore, arrange for a committee on worship from among its own members. The value of such a committee will be obvious upon a moment's reflection on how many elements are included in worship when it

is reverently and thoughtfully arranged. There is music involving organist and choir. Ushers should be carefully picked and trained. The sacraments must be regularly observed, calling for care of the utensils and preparation of the elements (this should invariably be arranged by ruling elders). Provision for filling the pulpit in the absence of the minister is another duty. Even the order of worship should not be left wholly to the minister although his judgment in such matters, based presumably on study and experience, should be carefully weighed. And to train people in the art of worship is equally the concern of both minister and elders. How enriching an experience for such a committee, and how profitable for the whole church if it might make constant study of all matters concerning congregational worship, devising ways and means whereby it might fulfill its function of bringing people " into the Holy Place " where Christ has entered to make a way for us.

3. The Christian education program in the church is under supervision of the session. From the very beginning of the church, witnessing and teaching have been its vocation: " Make disciples, . . . teaching them." The church should think of itself as a community of learners. Since its membership is composed of young and old, learning in the Christian teaching and way of life should include both children and adults. A committee on Christian education should be formed with responsibility for varied phases of the church's teaching mission. It may be wise to add to

the membership of this committee persons from the congregation who by experience and interest are well qualified to give valuable help. This committee will secure and sponsor the training of teachers and officers in the church school and provide leadership for youth organizations; it will prepare a budget adequate for the work of Christian education; it will arrange for youth participation in conferences; it will provide for missionary education and adult study classes; and it will recommend to the session whatever it deems necessary for the increase of knowledge in Christ. An enthusiastic and well-informed committee on Christian education can transform the character of the church. It is hardly fair to make a single individual, perhaps the superintendent of the church school, bear the entire burden. A wisely selected committee responsible to the session can give more adequate leadership to a program that will offer a learning opportunity for the entire church.

4. The session should be concerned also for the finances of the church. Sessions handle this responsibility in various ways. Frequently a finance committee of the session assumes duties that in other churches are performed by a board of trustees. In those instances where both a session and a board of trustees operate, a joint committee on finance representing each body may be set up to co-operate with each other and to correlate all financial matters. In any event the session cannot relegate to any other body responsibility for the benevolences of the congregation. For this

purpose a committee should be appointed which would perform several duties: (*a*) study the benevolence program of the denomination as authorized by the General Assembly; (*b*) propose the share of financial support the congregation will contribute; (*c*) so inform and interest the members that they will respond intelligently and generously. When we think of the budget of the church, the designation sometimes has been made of portions of it " for ourselves " and " for others." This is a doubtful distinction. We are a national and a world church; and our mission is *one* whether carried out locally, nationally, or world-wide. A session is known to have been unhappy about having a team from presbytery sent to inform it concerning the whole program of the Presbyterian Church on the ground that it did not need persons " from the outside " to instruct it! Our church is one; benevolences are as much " inside " business as paying the fuel bill! A good committee on benevolences and finance can make a church truly Presbyterian in its concept of unity with and obligation to the larger fellowship of which it is a part.

The committees mentioned above are merely suggestive. Sessions may wish to function with fewer or more or with different ones. In some churches supervision of evangelistic effort is assigned to a committee of the session; in others, stewardship education is made a special assignment. Flexibility of organization is very necessary if the necessities of contrasting situations are to be met. But what we have considered may give an indication of how a ruling elder may serve as a member of the session. He will probably work as a member of a committee but he will also have responsibilities of a more general nature. He must be willing to give sufficient time outside of meetings to these tasks. This he will be glad to do if he understands the nature and mission of the church. But unless he plans to include his service to the church among his other duties, he may not experience the true satisfaction and spiritual enrichment it will bring to him.

It may not be amiss to speak briefly concerning the discussion of subjects which come before the session. The same principle is true here as holds in other group conferences — there should be free and helpful participation by all present with ample time allotted for each matter. Ruling elders who are gifted conversationalists should take care lest through too frequent speaking they discourage those brethren who find it difficult to express themselves. The atmosphere of a session meeting should be warmly cordial, wholesomely serious, unregimented but orderly, and with openness to different points of view and to the leading of God's Spirit.

The church believes that God reveals his will through the Holy Spirit in groups of Christians who thoughtfully and prayerfully wait upon him for guidance. The session meeting should, therefore, provide for more than the business of the church; it should also give opportunity for spiritual growth through study and worship. Ruling elders themselves should be growing into the maturity that is in Christ. The Presbyterian Church is convinced that it can go no faster and no farther than the vision and knowledge of its officers will permit. So it has prepared, through the Board of Christian Education, splendid training courses which may be most profitably followed by the session of each church. Through study and conference together, under the leadership of the pastor, a ruling elder will thus enlarge his insight into the nature of the church, deepen his loyalty to Christ by a clearer discernment of Jesus' meaning for personal faith and the world's salvation, and will become a more effective and enthusiastic worker as he sees his part in the whole structure and program of the church.

So when you go to session meeting, go expectantly. You are part of that great company of Jesus' disciples of whom he said, " Greater works than these shall . . . [ye] do; because I go unto my Father."

V

THE CHURCHES
AND THE CHURCH

WHEN we think about organized Christianity (and has there ever been any other kind?), many of us will at once picture the particular church with which we are most familiar, probably the one of which we are members. We know it as a relatively small religious community carrying on its varied activities seemingly complete in and by itself. It is busy in a full life of worship, fellowship, teaching, and service which have come to have valued meaning to members through their participation. To all intents and purposes it appears autonomous in the regulation of its own affairs and in the ownership of property. Some denominations, which are " congregational " in form of government, define the Church (spelled with a capital " C " to distinguish it from the local congregation) as precisely all these individual churches entering voluntarily into co-operation with each other without, however, involving any curtailment of the sovereignty which inheres by right in each congregation.

The Presbyterian idea of the Church is quite different from this. The local organization is regarded as a member within the organism of the total Church. Churches are not independent and autonomous, but essentially and structurally each church is related to the larger body of which indissolubly it is a part. The Church and the churches are mutually involved in such a way that neither can exist without the other: the Church, indivisible and universal, must exist in the churches; but it is the faith vitally experienced in the churches which gives reality and power to the Church. This may seem very confusing, but it must be kept in mind because it is the idea on which the Presbyterian Church is organized. The local congregation, as just stated, is not autonomous. Although it is given a great deal of freedom in the determination of its own affairs, a moment's reflection will bear out that this freedom is exercised within well-defined limits set forth in our Form of Government. For instance, a congregation cannot by itself call and install its choice of a minister; it is the prerogative of the presbytery to approve the call, and to perform the act of installation. The minister holds membership not in a local church but in the presbytery. The minutes of session must be presented for examination to the presbytery, and all decisions and actions of a session or congregation may be reviewed by the presbytery. Presbytery has the ecclesiastical power to discipline a church, its session, or minister. Of the Presbyterian denomination we may properly sing, " All one body we," for we have one confession of faith, one consti-

tution and form of government, and one common
purpose. We recognize that in reality we are a closely
knit unity.

This unity we express through a representative
form of government. Each congregation through its
session is represented by a commissioner, or commissioners (where more than one minister is installed in
the church) in the presbytery. In turn, on a ratio
basis and in a balanced number of elders and ministers, each presbytery elects representatives to attend
the General Assembly. This is the highest court of
our denomination. Its jurisdiction extends over the
entire church. This system of government should not
be difficult for us in the United States to understand,
because in many respects there is a remarkable parallel between our government and church. Local units
of government approximate congregation and presbytery; and the Federal government, functioning
through legislative, executive, and judicial branches,
approximates the General Assembly with its various
ramifications. We hardly need to be convinced that
humanly speaking this is the best form of government! It expresses the unity and solidarity of the
whole, yet makes ample room for local independence
and initiative. Shall we boast that Presbyterians conceived this idea first! Let us see now how all this af-
fects a ruling elder who serves on the session of a
local church.

The session has responsibility for the benevolence
causes and budget of the local church. Every congre-

gation that is worthy the name of a Christian church should be doing something for others. It is a service agency carrying out the will of Christ. Its area of concern is not limited to its own life only but extends also to the community in which it is and to the wider needs of the nation and the world. No church will increase spiritual vitality within itself that is not growing in the range of its vision and outreach. To encourage the church in obedience to its Lord to undertake tasks beyond its own walls and to propose ways and means by which this shall be accomplished can be the most stimulating and exciting aspect of a ruling elder's work.

A notable New Testament scholar, speaking of the mission of the church, has said that its life and work should be a continuation of that which Jesus began to do in his short ministry on earth. In fact when we understand the church truly, it is itself a manifestation in the world of the present activity of the living Christ working through the Holy Spirit. The Gospels make it clear that our Lord conceived his work to be to preach the gospel of God, that is, evangelism; to teach the meaning of that gospel in relation to life; and to use his Spirit-given power to heal and help the needy. The church has always understood its mission in terms which it believed Christ himself had commissioned: " Go therefore and make disciples of all nations, . . . teaching them to observe all that I have commanded you; and lo, I am with you always, to the close of the age " (Matt. 28:19–20). So evangelism, teaching, and service in the name of Christ are the God-given tasks of the church. To carry out this mission the General Assembly has created agencies, responsible to it, which plan and administer the program in the area assigned to each.

1. One of these agencies is the Board of Christian Education. As its name implies, it is charged with responsibility for all phases of the teaching task of the church. Think of the tremendous challenge it faces and the amazing job it does! The Board prepares study courses and materials for students of the church schools ranging in age from little tots to aged adults. It conducts training schools in which each year thousands of leaders are given expert guidance in their various fields — church school teachers, young people's advisers, women's organization officers, and so forth. It sponsors hundreds of conferences for youth, vocational counseling, caravans, and program materials for Westminster Fellowships in which thousands of young people participate. It provides field service to make the teaching force in every church effective and a corps of expert directors of Christian education who visit churches for an extended period to vitalize the program of Christian education. It encourages high religious and academic standards in the more than twoscore colleges sponsored by the Presbyterian Church, and through the contributions made by the churches it supplies them with substantial financial support. It maintains Christian student centers adjacent to the campuses of the great universities of our

land where faculty and students gather for serious study, discussion, and faith-strengthening friendships. It provides in-service training for ministers who have been in the pastorate a few years so that they may be encouraged to maintain habits of study and improve their gifts and skills in the ministry. It devises courses of study for ruling elders so that they may gain competence in their work and joy in performing their duties. In short, whenever there is evident a need for teaching in any part of the church, there the services of the Board of Christian Education are called upon to meet the situation.

2. Another responsibility of the church is to make America Christian. As the first followers of Christ were commissioned to make disciples beginning " in Jerusalem, and in all Judea, and in Samaria " so we construe our duty to make Jesus Christ known and his will effective in every part and aspect of the life of our nation. Obviously this calls for a start right in the community in which we live. Every church should be aware constantly of the needs, not only of the local parish, but of the entire community. If there are other groups of Christians in the community, there should be co-operation between them in a united approach to common problems. Where there exists a council of churches, ruling elders should be active in its work. Presbyterians believe strongly in interchurch and interdenominational fellowship and action. On the national level, the Presbyterian Church belongs to the National Council of Churches and is eager to

show its unity with sister denominations through participation in the wider aspect of religious witness and service.

Yet the church also believes that it has its own great challenge to meet in making America Christian. So we have organized through the General Assembly a Board of National Missions charged with the responsibility to be the arm of the Presbyterian denomination in reaching all classes and groups in our country who need the ministry of the gospel. If a church were to trace its origins, as indeed many have, it would probably discover that somewhere in its beginnings the Board of National Missions had a part. The minister who first organized the church might have been sent by this Board; probably his salary for a time was paid by it. When the church's first building was constructed, the money might have been given or lent by the Board. The starting of new churches is still one of its major activities. But the Board of National Missions does not limit its labor to this alone; wherever there is need for the gospel and for Christian service, there the Board of National Missions is at work — among Indians, migrants, mountain people, immigrants to our shores, city slums, industrial chaplains, lonely ranchers on the plains or lonely settlers on Alaska's far frontiers — among all these our church has gone through its Board of National Missions.

3. The commission of our Lord clearly states also that we are to go into all the world. So we have or-

ganized the Board of Foreign Missions to carry responsibility for being the arm of the church stretching across the seas to bring the word and compassion of Christ to every nation. So wonderfully has God blessed this work that today there exists a universal church which is rooted with great strength and tenacity in every land. It was the aim of the missionary movement to make Christians, to gather them together in a mutually enriching and sustaining fellowship which should become self-supporting and self-propagating. That end has now been partially accomplished. As a consequence we no longer think of missions as " foreign," but we conceive a single worldwide mission of the whole church in which we also participate with our brethren of other races and tongues. We send " fraternal workers " upon invitation from sister churches, and we invite them to send leaders from their midst to visit among us in America. Foreign missions has become " world mission." Further, the Presbyterian Church contributes to world Christianity through active participation in the World Council of Churches.

Although there is this new look in missions, there is no indication that our help is not so much needed as ever. There are requests for more workers from America than our church is at present able to send — different categories of workers, doctors, teachers, dentists, agricultural experts, visual education and radio experts. The younger churches have not yet come to full self-support; our help is necessary in developing leadership through college training and vocational schools. We must also continue the ministry, in which our Lord was so engrossed, of healing the bodies of men, teaching child care, sanitation, proper diet, and so forth. If pride is permissible in Christians, the mission enterprise is something of which we may boast. Never has the church been so true to its vocation, never more worthy of praise, than in the heroic and unselfish service in which its missionaries have expended themselves for Christ in lands far from their homes and loved ones.

4. The Presbyterian Church does not forget its servants who have labored long and faithfully in its service. The Board of Pensions has been organized to care for these aged workers. An excellent pension system has been devised by the Board; relief to widows and needy ministers not adequately provided for is supplied; and oversight of homes for the aged is given.

It should be noted that all the Boards are set up in the same way. All are created by the General Assembly in answer to the church's need for an agency through which to extend its witness and work, all report annually to the church through the General Assembly, and each is administered by a professional staff responsible to a Board widely representative of the church and elected by the General Assembly. The Boards are in no way bureaucracies which function autonomously but are closely geared into the life of the church. On these Boards sit many of the same men and women who serve as ruling elders and leaders in the local church.

5. One other body that has been formed by the General Assembly should be noted although it functions in a manner quite different from that of the Boards which we have mentioned. This is the Council on Theological Education. As its name implies, it is concerned with training a ministry adequate for the present demands of the church. It co-ordinates the work of the nine theological seminaries in our denomination, sets up the budget for their partial support from the benevolence funds of the General Assembly, studies matters relating to the curriculum, and in general furthers the effectiveness of the institutions in which leadership for the church is trained.

6. Since the General Assembly meets only once a year and since it is not designed to be an administrative body which will carry through the program which it approves, the General Council has been formed to function between the meetings of the General Assembly, to study and plan the church's program on a long-range basis, and to expedite such matters as may be referred to it by its parent body. It has two main functions: to receive and co-ordinate the budgets of the boards and agencies of the church; and to administer a program by which the entire church may be informed and enlisted in the support of work committed by it to the Boards. Thus benevolence funds from the local church are sent to the central receiving agency which is administered by the General

Council. Here they are distributed to the various boards and agencies in accordance with allocations made by General Council, and approved by the General Assembly. The church is kept fully informed through a Department of Stewardship and Promotion of the needs of the Boards as they discharge the responsibilities committed to them. This eliminates overlapping and is an orderly way in which to present to the whole church its challenge and opportunity to evangelize, to teach, and to serve.

We may well take satisfaction in the very effective and well-articulated organization of the Presbyterian Church. But organization is useful only as it serves the life of the church. Since life is dynamic, organization must be dynamic too; and from time to time changes must be made. The structure of our church is firm, but elastic. Important modifications in doctrine or in structure can be made only by the entire church acting through decisions of a sufficient majority of concurring presbyteries. By this very wise provision, sudden and ill-advised innovations are discouraged, while thoughtful deliberation is given opportunity to form sound judgments and initiate constructive action.

This very rapid review of the way in which the Presbyterian denomination of which we are members carries out the Lord's commission to " make disciples of all nations, . . . teaching them," implies also that at every level ruling elders may be called upon to render service. As we have noted, the presbytery ordinarily, " consists of all the ministers, in number not less than five, and one ruling elder from each church, within a certain district." In anticipation of convening the presbytery, either at the stated time of such meeting or for a special purpose, notice is given to each minister and session and it then becomes incumbent upon each session to elect one of its number to represent it. Since presbytery is the nuclear unit of the Presbyterian form of government, it is important that the session shall elect able men to attend. It is unfortunate that sometimes the same ruling elders are sent principally because they may be those who can most conveniently go. The whole strength of the session should be represented in presbytery and the duty to attend if elected should be conscientiously fulfilled. In turn the presbytery annually will elect certain of its ministers and ruling elders to represent it at synod and at General Assembly. It should be made clear that these meetings are not conventions as generally understood, or promotional rallies, but are business and legislative assemblies where the work of the church is reviewed and where authoritative principles are established. It is therefore exceedingly important that the ablest ruling elders of the church should be willing to give time to them. It is heartening to note that ruling elders are increasingly taking places of importance in the organization of the church and its work and devoting valued time and labor in its behalf. The ideal toward which we strive should be a parity between ministers and ruling elders in the sphere of the spiritual government of the church based upon knowledge of and devotion to those matters which make for the " peace, unity, and purity of the church."

The Presbyterian Church is not sectarian in its point of view; that is, it does not hold a narrow or odd concept of the Christian faith, but is true to the broad spirit and ancient creeds of the church in all ages and in every land. This has resulted in the enthusiastic participation of our church in the National Council of Churches and in the World Council of Churches. The General Assembly appoints delegates, ministers and laymen, from our church to assemblies of these larger Christian bodies. Presbyterians are eager to promote union with other Christian communions and to this end maintain a permanent commission to encourage co-operation with them. It is our prayer that we all may be one even as our Lord desired, thus bringing healing and unity to our broken world. In these ever-widening circles we are privileged to make our witness and render Christian service.

VI
THE SESSION
AND THE PASTOR

And from Miletus he sent to Ephesus and called to him the elders of the church. — Acts 20:17. The strong bond of fellowship between the elders of the church in Ephesus and the apostle Paul gives intimation of the unique relation between the session and the pastor. The parallel is not exact because the apostle was not a settled minister in a parish. Yet on the occasion of a prolonged visit in the city during the course of a missionary journey, he doubtless had opportunity for extended collaboration from which grew the mutual esteem and love so movingly depicted in the incident described by Luke. There is no other enterprise in the world in which men are so drawn to one another and to the leader as in the labor which ruling elders and pastors undertake for their Lord and Savior. Friendship naturally develops where men are thrown together in common endeavors, and sometimes is unusually firm where special circumstances contribute to it; but this is a fraternity based upon the communion that Christ creates by his Spirit.

It is described in poignant words spoken by our Lord to his disciples: " You are my friends if you do what I command you. No longer do I call you servants, for the servant does not know what his master is doing; but I have called you friends, for all that I have heard from my Father I have made known to you. You did not choose me, but I chose you and appointed you that you should go and bear fruit and that your fruit should abide; so that whatever you ask the Father in my name, he may give it to you. This I command you, to love one another " (John 15:14–17). There are unhappy exceptions to the rule as might be expected among persons who are far from perfect; but rare is the situation in which a minister does not refer to " my ruling elders " with pride and affection, and conversely, ruling elders speak of their minister in equally warm terms.

The spirit of unity is not something that " just naturally happens "; it must be eagerly cultivated. (Eph. 4:2–3.) A few hints may be helpful in achieving this end.

1. As an expression of Christian principle the old adage, " Good fences make good neighbors," leaves much to be desired. Yet it does emphasize the truth that each of two parties must know and honor mutual rights and privileges if good relations are to be maintained. While it is a technical point, both ministers and ruling elders should know the limits of their respective authority and should not intrude upon the spheres assigned to each. For example, some phases

of his office a minister shares equally with ruling elders; indeed, because he exercises spiritual rule in the church he also is termed a " presbyter " or " elder." In this capacity his authority does not exceed that of a ruling elder; his vote in presbytery, synod, or General Assembly counts for no more than that of a lay commissioner. The parity is further emphasized in the fact that minister and ruling elders together compose the session and no action taken by either unilaterally is officially valid. But in other ways a minister stands in a quite different and unique relationship both to the session and to the congregation. It may not generally be known that a minister holds membership in the presbytery and not in the congregation which he serves. Furthermore, he is installed in the pastorate by the presbytery, to which is reserved the power to remove him from it. Thus it is evident that neither the session nor the congregation exercise authority over the minister. It ought also to be understood that the authority of the minister in the church does not rest in himself. In the Presbyterian order of church government, the presbytery exercises the office of bishop with oversight of each congregation and the minister is really the representative of presbytery, commissioned to serve a certain congregation. This status gives a minister considerable freedom, which under authority of the presbytery he must use to preach the gospel in its purity and fullness, and in love. A mutual respect for these provisions of our form of government will make for the

" good neighborliness " which is so great a blessing.

2. The observations that have just been made are not intended to imply that the session, or an individual ruling elder, should not consult with the minister in any matter concerning the church. Indeed, if he is a wise pastor, he will welcome the wisdom and guidance of the officers with whom he is so closely associated. Every minister can recall with gratitude instances where the sage counsel of an experienced Christian brother has prevented a rash act, secured balance in judgment, or brought perspective in a confused situation. In helpful ways the session can be the line of communication between pastor and people. Who can better know the congregation than the ruling elders elected to represent them? The session should have the concern and the courage to interpret the needs of the people to the minister as it sees them; the attitude of the minister should be so receptive that such observations will never be construed as reproaches. On the other hand, who has better opportunity to know the minister than those with whom he shares his office as elder? There often will be times when ruling elders should interpret to the people the hopes, the anxieties, and the points of view of the minister. When it may be impossible or unseemly for him to speak for himself, his brethren in the session who love him and trust him can most effectively do this for him. This mutual confidence and reciprocity is both fruit of the Spirit's work and condition of His further operation. This is in large measure the secret

of the fellowship of kindred Christian minds, which is like to that above.

3. No minister who is sensitive to the proprieties of his call and is unselfish in his motives will divulge to the congregation or to the session the great happiness that a little thoughtfulness on their part would bring to his family or himself. The minister and his family are constantly with people, yet they may feel a loneliness in the tasks to which they are called. The pastor bears the burdens of his flock, and the people may never know how great is their weight. The minister has his needs and his emergencies, and the ruling elders are in a better position than anyone else to know of these needs and these burdens. It is their privilege to help, individually as friends and fellow workers, and together in the session. No minister who is worth his salt will seek tokens of a people's affection and appreciation; but he too is human. His is a need for warm personal friendship for which professional relations, however proper and valued, are not enough.

4. At each celebration of the Lord's Supper our memory is stirred by reflection upon the presence of the Lord with his disciples on that occasion. Especially precious is this observance to ministers and ruling elders who unite in the performance of the ritual. It is no presumption for them to aspire to realize among themselves the wonderfully rich and deep comradeship which the disciples enjoyed who first partook of this sacred meal in the upper room. The

Communion table is so placed that the " official family " may gather about it. The minister officiates in the name of the unseen Lord, whose presence is no less real because " in the spirit." He gives the elements to the men who serve with him in the care of the people of God, who then distribute them to all worshipers present, as Jesus once broke bread and blessed it and by the hands of his disciples gave it to the multitude. No love can be deeper than the love of Him who said, " Greater love has no man than this, that a man lay down his life for his friends " (John 15:13) . Such in kind, however lamentably poor in quality, should be the love of a minister for his brethren. And as the Lord defined that " you are my friends if you do what I command you " so ruling elders will demonstrate their loyalty and esteem by following their minister " as they see him follow Christ." Typifying this unity in Christ, the minister and the ruling elders usually serve each other the elements, and in so doing dedicate themselves in the spirit of their Lord to minister to the people the benefits of his death. Here the relationship between minister and officers, and between both and the congregation are beautifully set forth. There is order, division of responsibility, and recognition of " honor to whom honor is due." But " Christ is all, and in all " (Col. 3:11) .

All that has been written in this handbook is based upon the premise that to serve as elder in the Presbyterian Church is a great honor and a rewarding service. But it is not the sort of honor desired by the world where one receives praise and plaudits; it is the satisfaction given to a man called by the Spirit through the voice of the church to serve Jesus Christ. The secret of his effectiveness will be a complete dependence on God, a wholehearted commitment to his responsibilities, and continuing growth. He will find that as he joins with his fellow elders in conferences and training experiences intended to promote development of his gifts, as he sincerely studies the will of God for his own life and usefulness, and as he faithfully carries out his duties to the people whose spiritual welfare is his concern, he will find worth and enduring satisfaction. This is a service which requires much and pays large dividends. May God bless all who are called to it.